United States Government Accountability Office

Report to the Subcommittee on
Tactical Air and Land Forces,
Committee on Armed Services,
House of Representatives

August 2013

ARMY NETWORKS

Opportunities Exist to Better Utilize Results from Network Integration Evaluations

August 2013

ARMY NETWORKS

Opportunities Exist to Better Utilize Results from Network Integration Evaluations

Why GAO Did This Study

In 2011, the Army began a major undertaking to modernize its tactical network to improve communication and provide needed information to soldiers on the battlefield. The Army has identified the network as its number one modernization priority requiring approximately $3 billion per year indefinitely. NIEs provide semi-annual assessments of newly developed systems. Given the importance of the network, GAO was asked to examine elements of the process the Army is using to acquire network capabilities. This report examines (1) the results of the NIEs conducted to date and the extent to which the Army has procured and fielded network solutions, and (2) Army actions to enhance the NIE process. To conduct this work, GAO analyzed key documents, observed testing activities, and interviewed acquisition and testing officials.

What GAO Recommends

To improve outcomes for the Army's network modernization strategy, GAO recommends that the Secretary of Defense direct the Army to (1) require successful developmental testing before moving to operational testing at an NIE, (2) correct issues identified during testing at NIEs prior to buying and fielding systems, (3) provide results to industry on Army's efforts to rapidly acquire emerging capabilities, and (4) pursue additional opportunities for collaboration with the test community on the NIEs. DOD agreed with the recommendations to varying degrees, but generally did not offer specific actions to address them. GAO believes all recommendations remain valid.

View GAO-13-711. For more information, contact Belva M. Martin at (202) 512-4841 or martinb@gao.gov

What GAO Found

Since 2011, the Army has conducted five Network Integration Evaluations (NIE), which have provided extensive information and insights into current network capabilities and potential solutions to fill network capability gaps. According to senior Department of Defense (DOD) test officials, the NIE objective to test and evaluate network components together in a combined event is sound, as is the opportunity to reduce overall test and evaluation costs by combining test events. Further, the NIEs offer the opportunity for a more comprehensive evaluation of the broader network instead of piecemeal evaluation of individual network components. However, the Army is not taking full advantage of the potential knowledge that could be gained from the NIEs, and some resulting Army decisions are at odds with knowledge accumulated during the NIEs. For example, despite poor results in developmental testing, the Army moved forward to operational testing for several systems during the NIEs and they demonstrated similarly poor results. Yet the Army plans to buy and field several of these systems. Doing so increases the risk of poor performance in the field and the need to correct and modify deployed equipment. On the other hand, the Army has evaluated many emerging network capabilities—with generally favorable results—but has bought very few of them, in large part because it did not have a strategy to buy these promising technologies. Army officials have stated that the success of network modernization depends heavily on industry involvement but, with few purchases, it is unclear whether industry will remain interested. Finally, the Army has not yet developed metrics to determine how network performance has improved over time, as GAO recommended in an earlier report.

The Army has several actions under way or planned to enhance the NIE process and has further opportunities to collaborate with the test community. The Army has identified issues in the NIE process and its network modernization strategy that were causing inefficiencies or less-than-optimal results and has begun implementing actions to mitigate some of those issues. For example, the Army has begun performing technology evaluations, and integration of vendor systems in a lab environment to weed out immature systems before they get to the NIE. The Army has also developed a strategy and has an acquisition plan to address requirements, funding, and competition issues that will help enable it to buy emerging capabilities rapidly. However, the Army will need to validate the new strategy and plan and provide results to industry, which could help to manage industry expectations about how many of and how quickly it can buy these capabilities. DOD has started to identify and evaluate network metrics and to re-focus NIEs to gather additional data and insights. Taking these actions will ultimately allow the periodic review and evaluation of the actual effectiveness of network capabilities and the likely effectiveness of proposed investments. The test community has worked closely with the Army on the NIEs but has also voiced various concerns about the NIEs including their being a schedule-driven event. Tension between the acquisition and test communities has been long-standing. Additional opportunities exist for Army leadership and the test community to work together to further improve NIE execution and results and to reduce tensions between the two communities. A good starting point for the Army would be to take a fresh look at the test community observations and recommendations from previous NIEs.

_____ United States Government Accountability Office

Contents

Abbreviations

ATEC	US Army Test and Evaluation Command
BMC	Army Brigade Modernization Command
DOD	Department of Defense
DOT&E	Director, Operational Test and Evaluation
DT&E	Developmental Testing and Evaluation
GAO	US Government Accountability Office
JTRS	Joint Tactical Radio System
NIE	Network Integration Evaluation
OSD	Office of the Secretary of Defense
SUE	System under Evaluation
SUT	System under Test
USD (AT&L)	Under Secretary of Defense for Acquisition, Technology, and Logistics
WIN-T	Warfighter Information Network - Tactical

GAO U.S. GOVERNMENT ACCOUNTABILITY OFFICE

441 G St. N.W.
Washington, DC 20548

August 22, 2013

The Honorable Michael R. Turner
Chairman
The Honorable Loretta Sanchez
Ranking Member
Subcommittee on Tactical Air and Land Forces
Committee on Armed Services
House of Representatives

In 2011, the Army began a major undertaking to modernize its tactical network—at an estimated cost of about $3 billion per year indefinitely—to improve communication and other capabilities and to provide needed information to soldiers and commanders on the battlefield. The Army has identified this network as its number one modernization priority. For nearly 20 years, the Army has had limited success in developing its information network of sensors, software, and radios to give soldiers and commanders exact information when they need it, in any environment, and thus improve situational awareness and decision making in combat. To achieve this goal, the Army is implementing a new agile process,[1] which would take advantage of emerging networking solutions to keep better pace with technology development and deploy selected systems to the field much faster than previously possible. One key component of this process is the Network Integration Evaluations (NIE), which are assessments of newly developed systems held twice a year. The systems are included in brigade level military exercises, which help Army senior leaders decide whether the Army should field new systems.

The NIEs have several functions. They provide critical operational test information for systems developed by the government, as well as evaluations of commercially developed systems to fill network capability gaps identified by the Army.[2] During the NIEs, the Army integrates new systems before fielding to lessen the associated burden on operational forces. NIEs also help the Army perform a comprehensive evaluation of

---

[1]The Army's agile capabilities life-cycle process should not be confused with the agile software development approach for information technology systems. The Army's agile process is being used, at least initially, to identify and evaluate new networking capabilities for brigade combat teams.

[2]Capability gaps are identified unfulfilled capability needs.

new systems in an environment that models actual battle, resulting in recommendations by soldier and system evaluators on whether to field, continue to develop, or discontinue evaluation of these systems.

Because of the network's importance, the ambitious nature of the current network modernization strategy, and the department's history with system acquisitions over the past decade, you asked us to examine elements of the new process the Army is using to acquire network capabilities. We will address issues related to the NIE process, evaluation of new and current network capabilities, and current plans for major network acquisition programs in phases. In our first report, we addressed issues related to the Army's agile process.[3] In this report, we examine the Army's NIEs, a key enabler of the agile process. Specifically, we evaluated (1) the results of the NIEs conducted to date and to what extent the Army has procured and fielded proposed network solutions; and (2) Army actions and additional opportunities to enhance the NIE process.

To conduct this work, we used DOD policies and acquisition best practices as a guide as we evaluated the Army's approach to the NIEs and their contributions to modernizing its tactical network. We observed testing, visited laboratory facilities, interviewed acquisition and test officials, and analyzed key documentation. A detailed description of our scope and methodology is included in appendix I.

We conducted this performance audit from September 2012 to August 2013 in accordance with generally accepted government auditing standards. Those standards require that we plan and perform the audit to obtain sufficient, appropriate evidence to provide a reasonable basis for our findings and conclusions based on our audit objectives. We believe that the evidence obtained provides a reasonable basis for our findings and conclusions based on our audit objectives.

Background

As the Army transitions away from major wartime operations, it faces fiscal constraints and a complex and growing array of security challenges. The Army will be smaller and senior leaders recognize that the core of a smaller yet still highly capable force is having a capable tactical information network.

---

[3]GAO, *Army Networks: Size and Scope of Modernization Investment Merit Increased Oversight,* GAO-13-179 (Washington, D.C.: Jan. 10, 2013).

Over the last decade, the Army focused most of its decisions to field network improvements on supporting operations in Iraq and Afghanistan, an effort that was both expensive and time consuming. The Army did not synchronize the development and fielding efforts for network technologies. Funding and time lines for network-related programs were rarely, if ever, aligned. The Army fielded capabilities in a piecemeal fashion and the user in the field was largely responsible for integrating them with existing technology.

In December 2011, Army leaders finalized the Network-enabled Mission Command Initial Capabilities Document, a central document that describes the essential network capabilities required by the Army as well as scores of capability gaps. These capabilities support an Army mission command capability defined by a network of command posts, aerial and ground platforms, manned and unmanned sensors, and dismounted soldiers linked by an integrated suite of mission command systems. A robust transport layer capable of delivering voice, data, imagery, and video to the tactical edge (i.e., the forward battle lines) connects these systems.

To achieve the objectives of its network modernization strategy, the Army is changing the way it develops, evaluates, tests, and delivers networked capability to its operating forces, using an approach called capability set management. A capability set is a suite of network components, associated equipment, and software that provides an integrated network capability.[4] A requirement is an established need justifying the allocation of resources to achieve a capability to accomplish military objectives. Instead of developing an ultimate capability and buying enough to cover the entire force, the Army plans to buy only what is currently available, feasible, and needed for units preparing to deploy. Every year, the Army will integrate another capability set that reflects changes or advances in technology since the previous set. To support this approach, the Army is implementing a new agile process that identifies capability gaps and solicits solutions from industry and government to evaluate during the NIEs.[5]

---

[4]Army officials refer to network capabilities planned for fielding in 2013 as capability set 13.

[5]NIEs are sequentially numbered—NIE 14.1 and 14.2 are the two events scheduled to occur in fiscal year 2014.

GAO-13-711 Army Networks

NIEs are a significant investment. Since 2011, the Army has conducted five of them, and has projected the cumulative cost of the events at $791 million.[6] The Army conducts NIEs twice a year. Each NIE typically involves around 3,800 soldiers and 1,000 vehicles, and up to 12,000 square kilometers of territory, and approximately 6 weeks in duration. The two categories of the key participating systems during the NIEs are Systems under Test (SUT) and Systems under Evaluation (SUE), and each is subject to differing levels of scrutiny.

- SUTs are from an ongoing acquisition program (sometimes referred to as a program of record) that are formally determined to be ready for operational testing in order to inform an acquisition decision.[7] This operational testing is subject to review and is conducted with the production or production-like system in realistic operational environments, with users that are representative of those expected to operate, maintain, and support the system when fielded or deployed.

- SUEs are provided by either industry or the government. They are either (1) developing capabilities with sufficient technology, integration, and manufacturing maturity levels to warrant NIE participation; or (2) emerging capabilities that are seen as next generation war-fighting technologies that have the potential to fill a known gap or improve current capabilities. SUEs are not subject to formal test readiness reviews, nor the same level of testing as the SUTs. SUEs are operationally demonstrated and receive a qualitative user evaluation, but are not operationally tested and are not the subject of a formal test report (as SUTs are).

Aside from their role in the agile process, NIEs also provide the Army with opportunities for integration, training, and evaluation that leads to doctrine, organization, training, materiel, leadership and education, personnel, and facilities recommendations; and the refinement of tactics, techniques, and procedures related to the systems tested.

---

[6]The Army also conducted a preliminary network demonstration in fiscal year 2011 at a cost of $195 million.

[7]An acquisition program is a directed, funded effort that provides a new, improved, or continuing materiel, weapon or information system, or service capability in response to an approved need.

The Army believes that traditional test and evaluation processes frequently result in fielding outdated technologies and expects to improve on those processes through the NIEs. The Army's test community members, including the Brigade Modernization Command (BMC) and the Army Test and Evaluation Command (ATEC), conduct the testing during the NIEs. The BMC is a headquarters organization within the Training and Doctrine Command. It has an attached operational 3,800-soldier brigade combat team dedicated to testing during the NIEs. BMC soldiers use systems during the NIE in simulated combat scenarios for testing and evaluation purposes, resulting in qualitative evaluations based on their observations. The BMC also recommends whether to field, continue developing, or stop developing each solution and to improve the integration of capabilities into deploying brigades. ATEC has overall responsibility for the planning, conduct, and evaluation of all Army developmental and operational testing. ATEC also produces a qualitative assessment of the overall performance of the current capability set of network equipment.

Two test offices within the Office of the Secretary of Defense that help inform Defense Acquisition Executive decisions also provide oversight on testing related to major defense acquisition programs. The Director, Operational Test and Evaluation (DOT&E) provides oversight of operational testing and evaluation for SUTs. The Deputy Assistant Secretary of Defense for Developmental Test and Evaluation (DT&E) provides oversight of developmental testing that precedes operational testing of SUTs. DOT&E and DT&E roles are limited to the SUTs selected for operational testing during the NIEs.

Test and evaluation is a fundamental aspect of defense acquisition. DOD, under its Defense Acquisition System, requires the integration of test and evaluation throughout the defense acquisition process to provide essential information to decision makers; assess attainment of technical performance parameters; and determine whether systems are operationally effective, suitable, survivable, and safe for intended use.[8] Testers generally characterize test and evaluation activities as either developmental or operational. Developmental testing is a generic term

---

[8]Operational effectiveness is the overall degree of mission accomplishment of a system when used by representative personnel in the environment expected. Operational suitability is the degree to which a system can be used and sustained satisfactorily in the field. Survivability factors consist of those system design features that reduce the risk of fratricide, detection, and the probability of being attacked.

encompassing modeling and simulation and engineering type tests that are used to verify that design risks are minimized, that safety of the system is certified, that achievement of system technical performance is substantiated, and that readiness for operational test and evaluation is certified. The intent of developmental testing is to demonstrate the maturity of a design and to discover and fix design and performance problems before a system enters production.

Operational testing is a field test of a system or item under realistic operational conditions with users who represent those expected to operate and maintain the system when it is fielded or deployed. Specific operational tests include limited user tests, initial operational tests, and customer tests. Before operational tests occur for major acquisition programs, DT&E completes an independent Assessment of Operational Test Readiness.[9] Each Assessment of Operational Test Readiness considers the risks associated with the system's ability to meet operational suitability and effectiveness goals. This assessment is based on capabilities demonstrated in developmental testing. The Defense or Component Acquisition Executive considers the results of the Assessment of Operational Test Readiness, among other inputs, in making decisions on a major acquisition program proceeding to operational testing.

Army Not Taking Full Advantage of Potential Knowledge from NIEs

The Army has made steady improvements in the NIE process since its inception and the evaluations continue to give the Army useful information and helpful insights into current and emerging networking capabilities. However, some resulting Army decisions are at odds with knowledge produced during the NIEs. Most importantly, despite poor operational test results for a number of SUTs during the NIEs, the Army has sought approval to buy additional quantities and field several major networking systems. While many of the SUEs received favorable reviews, the Army lacked a strategy that addresses a number of procurement barriers—such as funding availability and requirements—when it began the NIE process, which precluded rapid procurement of successful SUEs. Additionally, as we reported previously, the Army has not yet tapped into the potential to

---

[9]Assessments of Operational Test Readiness are now called Developmental Test and Evaluation Assessments.

use the NIE to gain insight into the effectiveness and performance of the overall tactical network.[10]

NIEs Provide Several Advantages and Produce Volumes of Potentially Useful Information

To date, the Army has conducted five NIEs, costing an average of $158 million to plan and execute. Through those five NIEs, the Army has operationally tested 19 SUTs and evaluated over 120 SUEs.

NIEs have helped the Army in a number of ways. The NIEs allowed the Army to

- formulate a network architecture baseline that will serve as the foundation upon which the Army plans to add networking capabilities in the future;

- evaluate industry-developed systems that may help address Army-identified capability gaps in the future;

- integrate the new capability sets into operational units and to create new tactics, techniques, and procedures for using the new systems in operations; and

- provide soldiers with an opportunity to both provide input into the designs of networking systems and to integrate the systems before the Army fields them to operational brigades.

According to Army officials, testing during each NIE generates a large volume of potentially useful information. There are detailed operational test and evaluation reports for each of the SUTs, user evaluations for each of the SUEs, an integrated network assessment of the current capability set, and general observations on the NIE event itself.

The DOT&E has reported observations of the NIEs in its fiscal years 2011 and 2012 annual reports, including an overall assessment, operational scenarios and test design, threat information operations, and logistics. According to DOT&E, the intended NIE objective to test and evaluate network components together in a combined event is sound, as is the opportunity to reduce overall test and evaluation costs by combining test events. NIEs also offer the opportunity for a more comprehensive evaluation of a mission command network instead of piecemeal

---

[10]GAO-13-179.

evaluation of individual network components. In addition, the DOT&E generally reported overall improvements in the execution of the NIEs, realistic and well-designed operational scenarios, and improvements in threat information operations.

ATEC, in addition to preparing operational test reports for specific systems, also prepares an integrated network assessment after each NIE. The reports attempt to characterize how well the current capability set performed with respect to several essential capabilities the Army needs for improved mission command. Based on the performance characterizations presented in the available reports for all NIEs, it appears the Army is making progress in improving its networking capabilities. For instance, the integrated network assessments for NIEs 12.2 and 13.1 cited improvements in an essential capability called network operations. These reports also showed improvements in the common operating picture, which is a capability that enables the receipt and dissemination of essential information to higher echelon command posts. As the Army has modified the reports to improve how they present both capability set performance and essential capabilities, the reports have become tools that are more useful for decision makers.

Army Accepting Risk by Buying and Fielding Systems with Poor Operational Test Results During the NIEs

Four SUTs that the Army plans to buy and field as part of capability set 13—Warfighter Information Network-Tactical (WIN-T) Increment 2, Joint Tactical Radio System Manpack Radio, Joint Tactical Radio System Rifleman Radio, and Nett Warrior—have demonstrated continued poor performance and/or reliability in both developmental tests before NIEs and operational tests during the NIEs. According to the DOT&E, system development best practices dictate that a system should not proceed to operational testing until it has completed developmental testing and corrected any identified problems. To address these problems, the Army has taken steps to implement design changes and schedule additional testing to verify performance after it has implemented those changes. However, in doing so, the Army faces the risk of making system design changes during the production phase or fielding systems with less than required performance or reliability.

Two of these SUTs performed poorly during developmental testing. Developmental testers, through their Assessment of Operational Test Readiness reports, recommended that the Manpack Radio and the Rifleman Radio not proceed into operational testing. Despite these recommendations, the Army proceeded with initial operational testing for these systems during NIEs while reclassifying the participation of other systems as either limited user tests or customer tests. The outcomes were predictably poor, according to DOT&E. See table 1 for operational test results from ATEC and DOT&E reports.

Table 1: Operational Test Results for Five Networking Systems

System	Description	Operational effectiveness	Operational suitability	Survivability
WIN-T Inc 2	The Army's high-speed and high-capacity backbone communications network. Increment 2 is intended to provide command and control on-the-move down to the company level for maneuver brigades and implements improved network security architecture.	Not effective. Key software waveforms[a] and a tactical relay tower not operationally effective in NIE 13.1. At speeds over 25 miles per hour, information throughput capability decreased significantly. However, soldiers said they would still prefer to deploy with the system as it provides a capability that the Army cannot currently provide to soldiers in theater.	Not suitable. Six of eight configuration items did not meet reliability or availability requirements.	Not survivable, did not protect network from outside penetration.
Joint Tactical Radio System Manpack Radio	A two-channel software-defined radio that is intended to interoperate with existing legacy radios and increase communications and networking capabilities.	Not effective. Poor performance of legacy waveform.	Not suitable. Did not meet reliability or availability requirements.	(Not discussed in test report summary)
Joint Tactical Radio System Rifleman Radio	A one-channel handheld software-defined radio that is intended to operate the soldier radio waveform.	Rated effective for platoon operations	Not suitable. Did not meet reliability requirements in Initial Operational Test and Evaluation.	(Not discussed in test report summary)
Nett Warrior	Leverages commercial smart devices and secure Army tactical radios to provide the dismounted leader an integrated mission command and situational awareness system for use during combat operations.	The utility and support provided by Nett Warrior varied by leader and by task.	Suitable in Limited User Test. Exceeded reliability and availability requirements.	Light emission compromises leaders' survivability at night.
Joint Battle Command-Platform	Intended to generate and disseminate mission command and situational awareness messages.	Not effective. Displays showed inaccurate information.	Not suitable. Poor reliability during testing (82 hours vs. 470 hours requirement). Key configuration was not a fieldable system.	Not survivable. Significant information assurance issues when threat forces are present.[b]

Source: ATEC and DOT&E (data); GAO (presentation).

[a]A waveform is the representation of a signal that includes the frequency, modulation type, message format, and/or transmission system.

[b]Information assurance includes those measures that defend and protect information and information systems by ensuring their confidentiality, integrity, authenticity, availability, and utility.

In its 2012 annual report, DOT&E pointed out that proceeding to operational testing only confirmed the deficiencies identified in developmental testing. For example, the WIN-T Increment 2 system's reliability was troublesome enough in a limited user test to warrant a reduction in the reliability requirement. However, WIN-T Increment 2 was unable to meet the reduced requirement. The Rifleman Radio also demonstrated poor reliability during developmental testing in 2011 and even worse reliability in operational testing due to the enhanced stress of an operational environment. The DOT&E stated in its 2012 annual report that, according to system development best practices, the Army should not proceed to an Initial Operational Test and Evaluation with a system until it has completed developmental testing and the program has corrected any identified problems. Otherwise, the Army may conduct costly operational tests that simply confirm developmental testing conclusions about poor system performance and reliability rather than taking action to fix system shortfalls. Further, DOT&E's 2012 annual report was critical of the Army's NIE schedule-driven approach, which elevates meeting a schedule above adequately preparing a system to achieve success in operational testing. An event-driven approach, conversely, would allow systems to participate in a test event after the systems have satisfied certain criteria. Under the Army's schedule-driven approach, the NIEs are held twice a year and SUTs must align their operational testing to coincide with the next available NIE. An event driven-approach—versus a schedule-driven approach—is the preferred method of test scheduling. Using a schedule-driven approach can result in fielding systems that do not provide adequate utility for soldiers and require costly and time-consuming modification in theater.

Army Working to Address Performance and Reliability Issues Identified During NIE

In light of poor operational test results during previous NIEs, the Army now must pay for and conduct additional, unanticipated, tests to improve system performance and reliability. The extent to which the additional tests corrected all of the identified problems is unknown at this time as the Army awaits the results of the operational testing conducted at the most recent NIE. Ideally, the Army would demonstrate greater levels of operational effectiveness and suitability prior to making production and fielding decisions. Both GAO and DOT&E have acknowledged the risks of proceeding through testing, and to procurement, with systems that perform poorly.[11] Such systems often require design changes that

---

[11]GAO, *Defense Acquisitions: Assessments of Selected Weapon Programs,* GAO-13-294SP (Washington, D.C.: March 28, 2013).

frequently happen when systems are already in production, which can be more costly and technically challenging. Table 2 summarizes the additional activities required of selected systems.

Table 2: Additional Activities Required to Correct Performance and Reliability Issues for Selected SUTs

System	Description	Operational effectiveness	Operational suitability	Survivability
WIN-T Inc 2	The Army's high-speed and high-capacity backbone communications network. Increment 2 is intended to provide command and control on-the-move down to the company level for maneuver brigades and implements improved network security architecture.	The Army conducted a developmental test event at the contractor facility to demonstrate actions to correct issues found in testing and conducted lab-based risk reduction events to further characterize and analyze corrective actions. Army used NIE 13.1 results to confirm improved performance in an operational environment.	The Army revised the system's projected reliability growth (which the Defense Acquisition Executive subsequently approved); executed two reliability test events to identify and correct new failure modes; updated its training material; and provided refresher training to the test unit. Army used NIE 13.1 to demonstrate increased reliability and plot growth in system reliability.	The Army has executed lab testing to identify vulnerabilities and conducted additional survivability testing to demonstrate and validate information assurance fixes.
Joint Tactical Radio System Manpack Radio	A two-channel software-defined radio that is intended to interoperate with existing legacy radios and increase communications and networking capabilities.	The Army has implemented software improvements that have increased performance of both the legacy waveform and the operating system. Future testing will verify these corrective actions.	The Army is addressing failures found in operational testing to improve reliability.	The system's test report summary contained no survivability issues.
Joint Tactical Radio System Rifleman Radio	A one-channel handheld software-defined radio that is intended to operate the Soldier Radio Waveform.	System rated effective for platoon operations	The Army has continued updating software to increase reliability; improved training and troubleshooting procedures; and conducted additional testing. Army states that the Nett Warrior system—which is to be used in conjunction with the Rifleman radio—has now surpassed a key reliability requirement.	The Army reported no issues in the system's test report summary,
Joint Battle Command-Platform	Intended to generate and disseminate mission command and situational awareness messages.	The Army conducted a government developmental test to fix and verify inaccurate information display issues discovered during NIE 13.1.	The Army is clarifying the overall reliability requirement in the Capability Development Document. The Army is also deferring the demonstration of a beacon capability, which allows for situational awareness and vehicle tracking, until NIE 14.2.	The Army has corrected information assurance issues and validated fixes during a formal government development test.

Source: U.S. Army and DOD (data); GAO (analysis and presentation).

In addition to the unplanned testing summarized in Table 2 above, several systems have operational test and evaluation events scheduled. See table 3.

Table 3: Additional Testing Events Scheduled for Army Network Systems

WIN-T Increment 2	Follow-on Operational Test and Evaluation at NIE 13.2 to confirm correction of performance and reliability issues identified previously.
Joint Tactical Radio System Manpack Radio	Customer Test at Electronic Proving Grounds
Joint Battle Command-Platform	Initial Operational Test and Evaluation at NIE 13.2 to confirm correction of performance and reliability issues identified previously.

Source: U.S. Army (data); GAO (analysis and presentation).

Despite the poor test results and unplanned activities intended to improve SUT performance, the Army has begun fielding SUTs for capability set 13, including WIN-T Increment 2, Joint Tactical Radio System (JTRS) Manpack radio, Rifleman Radio, and Nett Warrior. Without disputing the test findings and their implications, Army leadership indicates that this equipment addresses critical capability shortfalls and operational needs by providing some level of capability that is otherwise unavailable. For example, most deployed units previously had no or very limited capabilities other than voice communications. Consequently, the Army believes it is urgent to modernize deploying units as quickly as possible, with the equipment in capability set 13.

The Army's approach carries risk. DOT&E has indicated that the principal way of operating a less reliable system is to invest more in recurring maintenance, which will enable the system to function, but will add to the program's life-cycle costs and increase its logistical support needs. As a result, the Army will likely have to work with a system that is less reliable than originally envisioned, and develop a new life-cycle cost estimate that reflects the added costs associated with the increased contractor support to keep this less reliable system operating. In addition, ATEC officials state that the negative impact of an individual system falling short of its reliability target is magnified in the capability set. This approach can result in fielded systems that do not provide adequate utility for soldiers and require costly and time-consuming modification in theater as well as additional testing. Our past work as well as reports from DOT&E and DT&E have all found benefits from adequate developmental testing prior to fielding to prove system performance.

Army Buying Few Systems under Evaluation, Despite Positive Soldier Feedback

Since the first NIE in 2011, the Army has evaluated more than 120 SUEs from both industry and government, many of which have received positive reviews and recommendations for fielding from the soldiers. However, the Army has been unable to buy many of these systems because it did not have a strategy in place to rapidly buy promising technologies. Army officials explained that existing DOD acquisition processes would not allow the Army to quickly acquire SUEs that could immediately address networking capability gaps. Even so, Army officials did not develop alternative acquisition approaches before they began the NIE process. It is unclear how long industry will continue to participate in the NIEs if the Army is unable to begin buying systems. As discussed later in this report, the Army has now developed new approaches to address barriers to its ability to quickly buy and field SUEs that have successful demonstrations during the NIEs.

Many SUEs have received positive reviews from soldiers at the NIEs—about five out of every six SUEs were recommended for fielding, field and continue development, or potential for follow-on assessment. Table 4 shows the range of soldiers' recommendations.

Table 4: Soldier Recommendations for Systems Evaluated during Each NIE

NIE	Field	Field and continue to develop	Potential for follow-on assessment	Do not field and do not develop	Inconclusive	Total
11.2	9	9	3	2	3	26
12.1	2	12	24	9	2	49
12.2	9	5	11	1	1	27
13.1	6	3	9	1	2	21
Total	26	29	47	13	8	123

Source: U.S. Army (data); GAO (presentation).

To date, the Army has decided to buy only three SUEs—a company command post, which is a collection of capabilities that enhances a company commanders' ability to plan, execute, and monitor operations; a touch screen-based mission command planning tool; and an antenna mast. The Army will field only one of these systems in capability set 13—the company command post. While Army officials tell us they would like to buy more systems, a number of factors—such as available funds, deployment schedules, system maturity, and requirements—determine which systems they can buy and when they can buy them. Because it did not have a strategy during the NIEs to address these factors, the Army has been limited in its ability to buy successfully demonstrated SUEs.

The Army expects industry participants to fund fully their own involvement and initial participation in the process and NIEs, which can be a costly endeavor. Army officials have said it can cost up to $250,000 for an interested contractor to provide a whitepaper for consideration. These whitepapers, which interested contractors submit to the Army in response to a sources sought notice, are the industry contractor's first opportunity to explain both their system and how it addresses a particular capability gap. The Army releases a sources sought notice to industry to solicit candidate commercial solutions for network/non-network capability gaps and the notice informs potential responders of evaluation criteria and subsequent NIE participation criteria. Participation in later phases of the agile process, and ultimately the participation in a NIE can cost the contractor an estimated million dollars, depending on the system the Army is evaluating. Because of the limited number of successfully demonstrated SUEs that the Army has purchased to date, and the cost associated with industry participation, there is concern that industry may lose interest. This could be especially problematic for the Army's agile process which, according to the Army, is heavily dependent on industry participation for success. Army officials remain confident in the continued support of industry, but the depth and longevity of this support is unclear at this time.

Army Not Using NIE to Evaluate Overall Network Performance and Effectiveness of Investments

While the NIEs are a good source of knowledge for the tactical network as a whole, the Army has not yet tapped into that potential. In January 2013, we reported the Army had not yet set up testing and associated metrics to determine how network performance has improved over time,[12] which limited the evaluation of the cost-effectiveness of its network investments. After completing each NIE, ATEC has provided an integrated network assessment of how well the current capability set enables the execution of the mission command essential capabilities. This qualitative assessment includes only the impact of the current capability set—and not the entire network—on the essential capabilities and does not attempt to evaluate the cost-effectiveness of the current capability set. The Army and DOD consider the fielding of capability set 13 as the initial output from the Army's network modernization portfolio, but the Army has yet to define fully outcome-based performance measures to evaluate the actual contributions of the capability set. Establishing outcome-based performance measures will allow the Army

---

[12]GAO-13-179.

and DOD to assess progress of network development and fielding and be in a position to determine the cost-effectiveness of their investments in capability set 13. We recommended that, among other things, the Secretary of Defense direct the Secretary of the Army to define an appropriate set of quantifiable outcome-based performance measures to evaluate the actual contributions of capability set 13 and future components under the network portfolio. As discussed later in this report, DOD has started to develop metrics in response to our earlier recommendation.

Army Actions and Additional Opportunities to Enhance the NIE Process

The Army is taking action to correct inefficiencies and other issues based on lessons learned from previous NIEs. The Army is also planning to address potential barriers to rapid procurement of successful SUEs, and DOD has started the process to implement our earlier recommendations on network metrics. Many of the initiatives are in the early stages of implementation so outcomes are not certain. The Army also has an opportunity to work more closely with the test community to further improve NIE execution and results.

Army Is Implementing Corrective Actions to Improve NIE Process and Network Modernization

The Army has identified inefficiencies or less-than-optimal results in its network modernization and the NIE process and has begun implementing corrective actions to mitigate some of them. Table 5 shows some of the major issues identified by the Army and the corrective actions, which are in early stages of implementation.

Table 5: Issues Identified by Army Officials and Corrective Actions

Issues	Corrective actions identified
Maturity of systems	To address issues relating to the maturity of SUEs, the Army screens vendor systems through a lab-based risk reduction process before acceptance for NIE participation. Army officials say this improves the test readiness of the SUEs.
Sources sought notices for potential vendors	Army officials said the initial NIE sources sought notice for NIE 12.2, which asked potential vendors to submit their proposed solutions, was too broad. This led to too many vendor responses being received that did not address the specific capability gap. A second, more targeted sources sought notice resulted in fewer submissions that were better targeted to the specific gaps according to Army officials.
Using vendors for NIE system integration	Army officials anticipate achieving future cost avoidance by having commercial vendors perform integration of new hardware before an NIE, such as putting new radios in vehicles.
System re-configuration capability	The Army has found that it needs the ability to automatically reconfigure radios and other systems remotely. Currently, these systems require intense pre-configuration and manual interface.
Information assurance	The Army has found increased demand for information assurance and protection as the number of network devices increases, requiring an active information security approach. (Army leadership has recently declared information assurance as an Army-wide priority.) Among the key issues are the manning and location of brigade information assurance capabilities.

Source: U.S. Army.

Note: Army refers to Army organizations other than ATEC.

The Army's lab-based risk reduction, currently under way, seeks to address concerns over too many immature SUEs sent to past NIEs. Through this initiative, the Army performs technology evaluations, assessments, and integration of vendor systems. Officials test systems individually and as part of an integrated network so that problems can be identified before proceeding to an NIE. In some cases, Army officials identify changes for these systems to increase the likelihood of their success during an NIE, while it drops others when they do not perform well enough in lab testing. Since this effort began, the Army has reduced the number of systems it evaluates during the NIEs, indicating the Army may be making soldiers' NIE workloads more manageable.

While Army officials acknowledge that lab-based risk reduction does not eliminate all risks, this early evaluation of new systems seems to address some concerns. It may reduce the number of immature systems in the NIE, which could help the Army train soldiers for the new systems. Sending only mature SUEs that have gone through integration testing to NIEs could also help avoid certain test costs.

Additionally, to reduce costs, improve the results of NIEs, and better support rapid fielding of new network capabilities, the test community has reported on several issues requiring corrective action by the Army. Additionally, the testers have also taken actions to help reduce redundancies in test data collection processes, among other things. Implementation of these corrective actions, which testers identified during earlier NIEs, could help prevent negative impacts to NIE testing and modernization. Table 6 describes a number of major issues identified by the test community and corrective actions, which are in early stages of implementation.

Table 6: Issues Identified by the NIE Test Community and Corrective Actions

Issues	Identified by	Corrective actions identified
Realism of operational scenarios	DOT&E	Test community officials indicate the Army is now using a more challenging set of NIE missions for soldiers to perform than were used in prior NIEs, and focusing more on Brigade-level operations rather than just smaller units.
Test data collection processes	ATEC	ATEC officials report they have reduced redundancies and inefficiencies in test data collection, allowing soldiers and testers to spend less time on these activities. They report improved processes for collecting data on system reliability, thereby allowing for higher fidelity test evaluations.
Integrated testing	ATEC	ATEC officials said they have integrated developmental and operational testing at the NIE, which allows costs to be avoided when compared to a more serialized approach.
Consolidate test support contracts	ATEC	ATEC officials reported consolidating its 5 test support contracts used for earlier NIEs into three contracts for NIE 13.1, helping them avoid about $36 million in costs. In the future, ATEC officials intend to further consolidate these three contracts into a single contract.
Test requirements	ATEC	ATEC officials reported avoiding about $10 million in costs by switching to a centralized approach to vetting test requirements within ATEC. They believe the Army needs to define more detailed operational requirements to assess industry-developed systems and make fielding decisions, and indicated this may occur in the future.
Training and guidance	ATEC and DOT&E	ATEC and other Army officials have identified a need for a more complete set of manuals, procedures (including digital standard operating procedures), training, and tactics to accompany new Capability Set systems. DOT&E officials said training modules appeared to overstate the proven capabilities of the Manpack radio.
Technical field support staffing	ATEC and DOT&E	Brigade Combat Teams receiving Capability Set 13 systems have identified a need for additional Army Signal Corps personnel to maintain the new equipment due to its volume and complexity. Similarly, ATEC officials found contractors at the NIE have to complete many soldier maintenance tasks, and that NIE contractor field support staffing is much higher than expected for Army units.

Source: ATEC and DOT&E.

Most of the corrective actions to address test community concerns are in early stages of implementation. Below are additional details about the status of a few of the key initiatives.

NIE Cost Avoidance Initiatives

Army test officials anticipate avoiding $86 million in NIE costs due to implementation of a dozen different efficiency initiatives, including making NIEs more efficient by eliminating duplicative surveys, consolidating data systems, refining SUE test data delivery processes, reducing reliance on contractor data collectors by using military personnel more, and automating data collection. Additionally, BMC officials indicated they intend to incorporate additional testing and reduce the number of soldiers involved in future NIEs to help reduce testing costs. Over time, as the Army conducts NIEs more efficiently, it plans to reduce the number of test personnel, realize commensurate salary savings, and reduce engineering expenses.

Training and Guidance

Training and guidance for soldiers using new systems during the NIE is another area receiving attention from the test community and the Army. Army test officials reported that there were gaps in soldier training for the SUEs to be evaluated in NIE 13.1. The training issues, in turn, affected the usefulness of the subsequent system evaluations. DT&E officials also expressed concerns about soldier training, and said problems exist in the rehearsal phase of the NIE process. Brigade Combat Team officials said they have also experienced a lack of training resources as they prepare to deploy overseas. According to Army officials, a lack of complete training information, tactics, techniques, and procedures is hampering soldier training on new network systems. That experience was somewhat mitigated, however, by help from soldiers who had used these systems during earlier NIE events. It will be important for the Army to resolve training issues before operational testers qualify systems as fully suitable for combat use following operational testing. Given that operations and support can often comprise about two-thirds of life-cycle costs, a good understanding of these requirements and costs will be necessary for the Army to make well-informed investment decisions for new equipment.

Assessing and using lessons learned from experience can help in planning and implementing future activities. The Army's efforts to reduce costs and implement corrective actions may take several years; therefore, a continued focus on making NIE processes more efficient and effective, as well as documenting the results of corrective actions would better support the Army's business case for conducting future NIEs.

Army Efforts to Reduce Barriers to Rapid Procurement of Successful Emerging Technologies

The Army is developing a two-pronged approach to address barriers to its ability to quickly buy and field SUEs that have successful demonstrations during the NIEs. According to Army officials, these barriers included a lack of well-defined requirements for the network system (instead of the more general capability gaps); a lack of funding; and lengthy time frames needed to complete the competitive procurement process. The Army found that the processes for translating capability gaps into requirements, identifying specific funding, and completing a competitive procurement can be very time consuming and challenging.

The Army is now developing a strategy to address these barriers. After the NIE, if the Army decides to buy and field a SUE, the Army plans to align that capability with a suitable existing requirement within an ongoing program of record. The selected program manager would then identify buying options for the capability, including the feasibility of using an existing contract, and would determine whether (1) funding is available, (2) the Army should identify the capability as an unfunded requirement, or (3) the Army needs an above-threshold reprogramming action.[13] The program manager would also determine if the Army can buy and field the capability in the capability set or identify what capability is achievable. Army officials plan to implement this new strategy in the coming months.

In cases where the Army cannot align the successful SUE with an existing program of record, it could develop a new requirement for the system. Army officials have indicated that in a small number of cases, the Army could utilize a directed requirement. The Army generally develops and approves directed requirements to fill urgent needs that the Army believes should be fielded as soon as possible. This allows for essentially bypassing the regular requirements processes, which require additional time to complete.

In addition to this strategy, the Army has developed a new NIE acquisition plan that features an alternative means to buy successful SUEs rapidly.[14] Under this new plan, the Army is using a combined sources sought notice and a request for proposals approach to better shape requirements and allow for buying SUEs in less time than under normal acquisition processes. With two NIEs per year, the Army will continue to use a sources sought notice to solicit government and industry solutions to broadly defined capability gaps and will assess those solutions during a

---

[13]Reprogramming is a utilization of funds in an appropriation account for purposes other than those contemplated at the time of appropriation. Reprogramming in amounts greater than certain thresholds, known as an above threshold reprogramming action, requires prior congressional approval. Department of Defense, Financial Management Regulation, 7000.14-R, Vol. 2A, Ch. 1, para. 010107.B.51 (Oct. 2008).

[14]On February 5, 2013, the Army submitted a report on this plan to the congressional defense committees in response to direction in House Report, H.R. Rep. No. 112-479, accompanying the House bill for the National Defense Authorization Act for Fiscal Year 2013, H.R. 4310.

NIE. Then, the Army will use lessons learned and soldier feedback from the first NIE to validate and refine the requirement and issue a request for proposal for participation in a future NIE. Using a request for proposal differs from using sources sought notices because the request for proposals approach culminates in the award of indefinite-delivery, indefinite-quantity contracts for industry SUEs to participate in a future NIE.[15] Using an indefinite-delivery, indefinite-quantity contract allows the Army to place production orders for industry SUEs following the NIE. The Army released the first request for proposals supporting a NIE on December 20, 2012, to solicit vehicle tactical routers for NIE 14.1. Vehicle tactical routers would allow users and systems located nearby to access networks securely.

For SUEs that already have a defined requirement, the Army plans to issue a request for proposals for participation in one NIE, without using a sources sought notice first. However, Army officials concede that a defined requirement is not usually available prior to the NIE. In those cases, the Army plans to continue issuing sources sought notices for industry proposed solutions that the Army will evaluate during a NIE, as a precursor to issuance of a request for proposals in the future.

The Army expects to comply with current DOD acquisition policy when it decides to buy systems that proceed through the agile process. However, the Army may propose changes to existing policy and processes that inhibit realization of the full benefits of the agile process.

As the Army implements this strategy over the coming months, it will be important to gather information on how well the strategy works and how rapidly the Army can procure and field a SUE after its successful demonstration during an NIE. At the same time, the Army will be in a better position to determine how much of its constrained budget it can devote to the procurement of SUEs. As recommended under internal control standards, it will be important for the Army to establish specific measures and indicators to monitor its performance and validate the propriety and integrity of those performance measures and indicators.[16] This type of information—on how many SUEs the Army can buy and how

---

[15]An indefinite-delivery, indefinite-quantity contract may be used when the exact times and exact quantities of future deliveries are not known at the time of contract award.

[16]GAO, *Internal Control: Standards for Internal Control in the Federal Government*, GAO/AIMD-00-21.3.1 (Washington, D.C.: November 1999).

rapidly—would be helpful for industry as it makes decisions on its future participation in the NIE process.

DOD Has Begun to Define Network Outcome-based Performance Metrics

In our initial report on the Army's tactical network, we concluded that it will also be important for the Army to assess the cost effectiveness of individual initiatives before and during implementation.[17] Moreover, to facilitate oversight, we concluded that it is important for the Army and DOD to develop metrics to assess the actual contributions of the initial capability set the Army will field in fiscal year 2013 and use the results to inform future investments.

According to a key DOD oversight official reporting on Army networks to the Under Secretary of Defense, Acquisition, Technology, and Logistics, DOD has started work to define quantifiable outcome-based performance measures for the Army tactical network. In addition, both DOD and Army officials indicated they are planning to develop a preferred end-to-end performance projection for the Army tactical communications network and intend to quantify the performance needed in terms of voice, data, and so forth, and by network tier, sector, and subnet. Officials plan to define levels of performance for benign and conflict environments and the waveforms and radios soldiers will need for each tier as well as their specific performance characteristics. Although this effort is in its early stages, this DOD oversight official stated that it is expected that the NIE will generate data on performance of the network as a whole, which could then be compared to the expected performance demand.

Separately, the Army is also beginning to prepare qualitative assessments of the progress the Army is making in filling capability gaps related to mission command essential capabilities. For example, ATEC has prepared an integrated network assessment after each NIE, which characterizes the level of capability achieved against the mission command essential capabilities. In addition, the Army has prepared a limited assessment of how capability set 13 will meet mission command essential capabilities.

Once the performance measures are in place and the Army evaluates the delivered capabilities against those measures, the Army will have the tools to evaluate the progress it is making and make any necessary adjustments to its investment strategy.

---

[17]GAO-13-179.

Opportunities for Additional Collaboration between Army and Test Community

The Army's network strategy features a variety of different approaches to testing and evaluation to accommodate the rapid pace of technology change and to reduce the cost and time of acquisition. The Army has worked closely with the test community to plan, conduct, and evaluate the NIEs. Also, as mentioned earlier, the test community has taken a number of actions to reduce the costs of planning and executing the NIEs. At the same time, the test community has been meeting its responsibility to objectively report on the tests and the results. However, test results for several network systems at the NIEs that did not meet operational and other requirements will result in added time and expense to address identified issues. An inherent value of testing is pointing out key performance, reliability, and other issues that need to be addressed as soon and as economically as possible, but not after fielding. DOT&E has stated that the schedule-driven nature of the NIEs contribute to systems moving to testing before they have met certain criteria.

Tension between the acquisition and testing communities has been long-standing. In that regard, the Defense Acquisition Executive recently chartered an independent team to assess concerns that the test community' approach to testing drives undue requirements, excessive cost, and added schedule into programs and results in a state of tension between program offices and the testing community.

One area the Defense Acquisition Executive assessment identified for improvement was the relationship and interaction among the testing, requirements, and program management communities. In that regard, the memorandum reporting the results called attention to four specific issues those communities need to address the

- need for closer coordination and cooperation among the requirements, acquisition, and testing communities;

- need for well-defined testable requirements;

- alignment of acquisition strategies and test plans; and

- need to manage the tension between the communities.

Concurrently, a systematic review of recent programs by DOT&E and DT&E examined the extent to which testing increases costs and delays programs. The results of both efforts indicated that testing and test requirements by themselves do not generally cause major program delays or increase costs. In addition, the Defense Acquisition Executive found no significant evidence that the testing community typically drives unplanned requirements.

Further, according to the DOT&E fiscal year 2012 annual report, three specific areas exist where increased test community interactions could result in improved test outcomes, which can result in systems with needed and useful combat capability being delivered to our forces more quickly. These include

- developing mission-oriented metrics to evaluate each system within the context within which it will operate;

- leveraging test and evaluation knowledge in setting requirements; and

- evaluating the multiple conditions in which the system is likely to be operated.

Additional opportunities exist for leadership of the Army and the test community to work together to further improve NIE execution and results. A good starting point would be for the Army to consider addressing the test community observations and recommendations from previous NIEs. Those included the schedule driven nature of NIEs, the lack of well-defined network requirements, and the lack of realistic battlefield maintenance and logistical support operations for SUTs during the NIEs. The Army is not required to and has not directly responded to the test community about its NIE observations and recommendations. Nevertheless, per internal control standards, managers are to, among other things, promptly evaluate findings from audits and other reviews, including those showing deficiencies and recommendations reported by auditors and others who evaluate agencies' operations.[18] In doing so, the Army may not only improve NIE execution and results but also reduce the tensions with the test community.

Conclusions

Within a sizable investment of an estimated $3 billion per year to modernize its tactical network, the Army is investing over $150 million per NIE to help ensure that those planned development and procurement investments result in the expeditious delivery of increased capabilities to the warfighter.

---

[18] GAO/AIMD-00-21.3.1.

The main product of the NIEs is knowledge. The Army has not consistently recognized, accepted, and acted upon the knowledge gained from the NIEs. On the one hand, the Army's fielding decisions to date seem driven by a pre-determined schedule rather than operational test results. Fielding individual systems that have done poorly during operational tests carries risk of less than optimal performance with the potential of costly fixes after fielding and increased operating and sustainment costs. Moreover, performance and reliability issues of individual systems could be magnified when these systems become part of an integrated network. On the other hand, even with a new strategy for procurement of emerging capabilities to fill capability gaps, the Army may still face an expectation gap with industry. The current constrained budget environment and the level of funding already allocated to ongoing network acquisition programs, may leave little funding to procure new networking technologies. Until it has clearly demonstrated the means to rapidly buy and field emerging capabilities and provided this information to industry, the Army may need to manage industry expectations of how many new networking systems it can buy and how rapidly.

The Army has implemented some lessons learned from planning and executing the NIEs. However, as part of a knowledge-based approach to its broader network modernization strategy, the Army should also be open to consideration of observations from all sources to improve process efficiency and achieve improved outcomes. We believe that the Army can and should collaborate more extensively with the test community on a variety of issues that could improve NIE outcomes. For example, as part of its responsibility to objectively conduct tests and report on their results, the test community has provided reports, observations, and recommendations before and following NIEs. To date, the Army has not directly responded to the test community's observations and recommendations on the NIEs.

Recommendations for Executive Action

To improve outcomes for its entire network modernization strategy, we recommend that the Secretary of Defense direct the Secretary of the Army to take the following four actions:

- Require that network systems from major defense acquisition programs obtain a positive Assessment of Operational Test Readiness (now called a Developmental Test and Evaluation Assessment) recommendation before being scheduled for operational testing during the NIE;

- Correct network system performance and reliability issues identified during the NIEs before moving to buy and field these systems;

- Provide results to industry on the Army's actual experience in buying and fielding successfully demonstrated systems under evaluation and the length of time it has taken to date; and

- Collaborate with all network stakeholder organizations to identify and correct issues that may result in improved network outcomes, including addressing the observations and recommendations of the test community related to the NIEs.

Agency Comments and Our Evaluation

DOD's written response to this draft is reprinted in appendix II. DOD also provided technical comments that were incorporated as appropriate.

DOD partially concurred with our recommendations that the Army (1) require network systems obtain a positive Assessment of Operational Test Readiness (now called a Developmental Test and Evaluation Assessment) recommendation before being scheduled for operational testing during the NIE and (2) correct network system performance and reliability issues identified during the NIEs before moving to buy and field these systems. In both cases, DOD states that processes are already in place to address these issues and that the recommendations as written take flexibility away from the Department. We disagree. Our findings indicate that DOD is not using its current processes effectively to evaluate a system's readiness to begin operational testing. While there may be instances where the Army uses operational testing to obtain feedback on system performance, DOD's system development best practices dictate that a system should not proceed to operational testing until it has completed developmental testing and corrected any identified problems.

The NIEs are a good forum for the Army to generate knowledge on its tactical network. However, NIEs are a large investment and DOD and the Army should strive to optimize their return on that investment. Approving network systems for operational testing at the NIEs after having poor developmental test results may not be the best use of NIE resources because of the strong correlation between poor developmental test results and poor operational test results. Moreover, it is much more cost effective to address performance and reliability issues as early as possible in the system development cycle and well in advance of the production and fielding phases. As we note in the report, DOD and the Army have been pursuing a schedule-based strategy for network modernization rather than the preferred event-based strategy where participation in a test event occurs after a system has satisfied certain criteria.

DOD concurred with our recommendation that the Army provide results to industry on how many successfully demonstrated systems under evaluation have been procured to date and how long it has taken for the procurements. However, DOD did not offer specific steps it would take to provide this information or a proposed timeframe. Because of the importance of continued industry participation in the development of the Army network, we think that it is important for industry to have a clear picture of the Army's success in rapidly buying and fielded emerging technologies. Finally, DOD concurred with our recommendation that the Army collaborate with all network stakeholder organizations to identify and correct issues that may result in improved network outcomes, including addressing the observations and recommendations of the test community related to the NIEs. DOD states that a collaborative environment with all stakeholders will assist in identifying and correcting issues and that the forum for doing so is the semiannual Network Synchronization Working Group. We agree that a collaborative environment is important in responding to previous test community observations and recommendations and would expect the Working Group to address these issues.

We are sending copies of this report to the appropriate congressional committees, the Secretary of Defense, the Secretary of the Army, and other interested parties. In addition, the report will be available at no charge on GAO's website at http://www.gao.gov.

If you or your staff have any questions about this report, please contact Belva Martin at (202) 512-4841 or martinb@gao.gov. Contact points for our Offices of Congressional Relations and Public Affairs may be found on the last page of this report. GAO staff who made key contributions to this report are listed in appendix III.

Belva M. Martin
Director, Acquisition and Sourcing Management

Appendix I: Scope and Methodology

Our objectives were to evaluate (1) the results of the Network Integration Evaluations (NIE) conducted to date and identify the extent to which the Army has procured and fielded proposed network solutions; and (2) Army actions and additional opportunities to enhance the NIE process. To address these objectives, we interviewed officials from the Army's System of Systems Integration Directorate; the Deputy Chiefs of Staff, G-3/5/7 and G-8; the Army Brigade Modernization Command, and the Army Test and Evaluation Command. We met with representatives of Army Brigade Combat Teams preparing for deployment. We also interviewed officials from the Deputy Assistant Secretary of Defense for Developmental Test and Evaluation; the Director, Operational Test and Evaluation; and the Office of the Under Secretary of Defense for Acquisition, Technology, and Logistics. We visited the Lab Based Risk Reduction facility at Aberdeen Proving Ground, Maryland and the NIE test site at White Sands Missile Range, New Mexico to meet with soldiers and civilian officials conducting testing.

To examine the results of NIEs conducted to date, we attended Network Integration Evaluations and reviewed test reports from the Brigade Modernization Command, U.S. Army Test and Evaluation Command, the Director of Operational Test and Evaluation, and the Deputy Assistant Secretary of Defense for Developmental Test and Evaluation. We reviewed briefing presentations for Army leadership that discuss test results and recommendations, and we toured lab facilities to understand how the Army is validating and selecting technologies for network evaluations. We reviewed Army programmatic and budget documentation to understand cost projections for testing and procuring network equipment under the new approach and we reviewed Army plans for resourcing this approach.

To identify actions and opportunities to enhance the NIE process, we interviewed Army officials to identify other networking challenges the Army is addressing concurrent with implementation of the agile process. We reviewed test results from both the Army and Department of Defense. We reviewed Army documentation identifying cost avoidance opportunities. We reviewed briefing information regarding lessons learned from activities related to the NIE, such as the screening and lab testing of candidate systems and soldier training. We spoke with officials at both Army and Department of Defense knowledgeable of lessons learned for the testing and fielding of new network capabilities.

We conducted this performance audit from September 2012 to August 2013 in accordance with generally accepted government auditing standards. Those standards require that we plan and perform the audit to obtain sufficient, appropriate evidence to provide a reasonable basis for our findings and conclusions based on our audit objectives. We believe that the evidence obtained provides a reasonable basis for our findings and conclusions based on our audit objectives.

Appendix II: Comments from the Department of Defense

ASSISTANT SECRETARY OF DEFENSE
3030 DEFENSE PENTAGON
WASHINGTON, DC 20301-3030

RESEARCH
AND ENGINEERING

AUG 9 2013

Ms. Belva M. Martin
Director, Acquisition and Sourcing Management
U.S. Government Accountability Office
441 G Street, N.W.
Washington, DC 20548

Dear Ms. Martin:

This is the Department of Defense (DoD) response to the GAO Draft Report, GAO-13-711,

"ARMY NETWORKS: Opportunities Exist to Better Utilize Results from Network Integration

Evaluations," dated July 12, 2013 (GAO Code 121098). Detailed comments on the report

recommendations are enclosed.

Sincerely,

Alan R. Shaffer
Acting

Enclosure:
As stated

GAO DRAFT REPORT DATED JULY 12, 2013
GAO-13-711 (GAO CODE 121098)

"ARMY NETWORKS: Opportunities Exist to Better
Utilize Results from Network Integration Evaluations"

DEPARTMENT OF DEFENSE COMMENTS
TO THE GAO RECOMMENDATION

RECOMMENDATION 1: To improve outcomes for its entire network modernization strategy, GAO recommends that the Secretary of Defense direct the Secretary of the Army to require that network systems from major defense acquisition programs obtain a positive Assessment of Operational Test Readiness recommendation before being scheduled for operational testing during the NIE.

DoD RESPONSE: Partially Concur.

Each DoD Component is required to establish an Operational Test Readiness Review (OTRR) process for programs on Office of the Secretary of Defense (OSD) operational test and evaluation oversight prior to any operational testing (OT). The Developmental Test and Evaluation (DT&E) Assessment prior to OT (previously referred to as the Assessment of Operational Test Readiness (AOTR)) is only one of several inputs that the OTRR uses to determine whether a program should proceed with OT. The process for assessing operational test readiness considers available information, including the associated risks, prior to deciding to conduct OT.

The recommendation as written takes flexibility away from the Department to send a program to an operational test (customer test, limited user test, etc.) to obtain early feedback on system performance from an operational unit. The Department has had success in bringing programs of record to an NIE early, and using Soldier and operational test feedback to change requirements and improve the program to better deliver needed capability or make system improvements. This approach has helped to reduce risk in later OT, delivered better products to the Soldier, and in some cases led to significant cost avoidance and savings.

RECOMMENDATION 2: To improve outcomes for its entire network modernization strategy, GAO recommends that the Secretary of Defense direct the Secretary of the Army to correct network system performance and reliability issues identified during the NIEs before moving to buy and field these systems.

DoD RESPONSE: Partially Concur.

The Department has a process in place to approve a program to proceed to the next phase in the acquisition cycle. The Milestone Decision Authority conducts a review to assess the results of initial operational test and evaluation, initial manufacturing, and initial fielding, and determine

2

whether to approve proceeding to full-rate production and/or full deployment decisions. Except as specifically approved by the Milestone Decision Authority, deficiencies identified in testing will be resolved prior to proceeding beyond low-rate initial production. Remedial action will be verified in follow-on test and evaluation.

The recommendation as written takes flexibility away from the Department to make program decisions. The Department continues to correct reliability, performance, and survivability issues identified during an NIE or other operational or developmental test venue. Soldier and lab-based risk reduction feedback from the NIE provides the foundation for a program manager's get-well strategy. However, correcting some performance issues may not be desirable from a cost or schedule standpoint.

RECOMMENDATION 3: To improve outcomes for its entire network modernization strategy, GAO recommends that the Secretary of Defense direct the Secretary of the Army to provide results to industry on its actual experience in buying and fielding successfully demonstrated systems under evaluation and the length of time it has taken to date.

DoD RESPONSE: Concur.

Results can be provided to industry, unless prohibited by regulatory and/or statutory requirements.

RECOMMENDATION 4: To improve outcomes for its entire network modernization strategy, GAO recommends that the Secretary of Defense direct the Secretary of the Army to collaborate with all network stakeholder organizations to identify and correct issues that may result in improved network outcomes, including addressing the observations and recommendations of the test community related to the NIEs.

DoD RESPONSE: Concur.

A collaborative environment with all stakeholders will assist in identifying and correcting issues that may result in improved network outcomes. The approved forum for addressing all NIE issues is the semiannual Network Synchronization Working Group, during which all Army elements and agencies, including the test community, are welcome to raise and address NIE-related issues to the community and Army leadership. The Army continues to work with the DoD test community to address concerns related to the NIEs.

Appendix III: GAO Contact and Staff Acknowledgments

GAO Contact

Belva M. Martin, (202) 512-4841 or martinb@gao.gov

Staff Acknowledgments

In addition to the contact named above, William R. Graveline, Assistant Director; William C. Allbritton; Marcus C. Ferguson; Kristine Hassinger; Sean Seales; Robert S. Swierczek; and Paul Williams made key contributions to this report.

GAO's Mission	The Government Accountability Office, the audit, evaluation, and investigative arm of Congress, exists to support Congress in meeting its constitutional responsibilities and to help improve the performance and accountability of the federal government for the American people. GAO examines the use of public funds; evaluates federal programs and policies; and provides analyses, recommendations, and other assistance to help Congress make informed oversight, policy, and funding decisions. GAO's commitment to good government is reflected in its core values of accountability, integrity, and reliability.
Obtaining Copies of GAO Reports and Testimony	The fastest and easiest way to obtain copies of GAO documents at no cost is through GAO's website (http://www.gao.gov). Each weekday afternoon, GAO posts on its website newly released reports, testimony, and correspondence. To have GAO e-mail you a list of newly posted products, go to http://www.gao.gov and select "E-mail Updates."
Order by Phone	The price of each GAO publication reflects GAO's actual cost of production and distribution and depends on the number of pages in the publication and whether the publication is printed in color or black and white. Pricing and ordering information is posted on GAO's website, http://www.gao.gov/ordering.htm. Place orders by calling (202) 512-6000, toll free (866) 801-7077, or TDD (202) 512-2537. Orders may be paid for using American Express, Discover Card, MasterCard, Visa, check, or money order. Call for additional information.
Connect with GAO	Connect with GAO on Facebook, Flickr, Twitter, and YouTube. Subscribe to our RSS Feeds or E-mail Updates. Listen to our Podcasts. Visit GAO on the web at www.gao.gov.
To Report Fraud, Waste, and Abuse in Federal Programs	Contact: Website: http://www.gao.gov/fraudnet/fraudnet.htm E-mail: fraudnet@gao.gov Automated answering system: (800) 424-5454 or (202) 512-7470
Congressional Relations	Katherine Siggerud, Managing Director, siggerudk@gao.gov, (202) 512-4400, U.S. Government Accountability Office, 441 G Street NW, Room 7125, Washington, DC 20548
Public Affairs	Chuck Young, Managing Director, youngc1@gao.gov, (202) 512-4800 U.S. Government Accountability Office, 441 G Street NW, Room 7149 Washington, DC 20548

www.ingramcontent.com/pod-product-compliance
Lightning Source LLC
Chambersburg PA
CBHW080640290526
45790CB00007B/3142